THE COFFEE SHOP CHRONICLES

By: Nevaeh Kirkland

The Coffee Shop Chronicles

Copyright © 2023 Nevaeh Kirkland

All rights reserved. No portion of this publication may be reproduced, distributed, or transmitted in any form or by any means, including photocopying, recording, or other electronic or mechanical methods, without the prior written permission of the publisher.

Printed in United States of America

First printing, 2024

Library of Congress Registration Number: TXu2400526

ISBN: 979-8-9891723-5-1

DEDICATION

This book is dedicated to my family and

a special thank you to my father

Albert Kirkland Jr.

Contents

CHAPTER 1: MY OVERWHELMING LIFE OF LONELINESSTIMES NEW ROMAN 1

CHAPTER 2: THE NIGHT, I MET HIM 4

CHAPTER 3: WHAT A DAY! 9

CHAPTER 4: THE FAIR 13

CHAPTER 5: T'S HOME 18

CHAPTER 6: WHO AM I? 24

CHAPTER 7: A CHOICE TO EMBRACE 28

CHAPTER 8: MORE OF THE UNKNOWN 32

CHAPTER 9: GRANDMA UNVEILS THE TRUTH 37

CHAPTER 10: T'S MIND BEGAN TO RACE 40

CHAPTER 11: VENUS WAKE UP 46

Chapter 1: My Overwhelming Life of Loneliness

I felt completely empty, like a dark cloud was smothering any hint of emotion or connection inside me. It seemed as if I were just existing—a lost figure in a world teeming with life. Often, I wondered about the purpose of my existence, but every time I considered escaping this pain, I couldn't muster the courage to act on those thoughts. It felt like the universe was determined to keep me stuck in this suffocating existence.

My life felt hollow, lacking meaning, with no excitement. My grandmother, preoccupied with her own issues, remained unaware of my silent suffering. It was as if I were an invisible soul, unseen by those around me, forced to grapple with loneliness and sadness on my own. My mother had passed away when I was born, and my father's identity remained a mystery. I carried the weight of abandonment and isolation like a heavy burden, pulling me deeper into the depths of despair.

I couldn't bring myself to seek assistance from a counselor or psychologist, convinced I could navigate my tangled thoughts without help. I didn't think anyone would understand, so I chose isolation, believing I could endure my challenges without burdening others. Deep down, I guess I just wanted to feel loved and not alone in this big world. For the moment, I was wandering through the wilderness of my own sorrow.

I had a job at a cozy coffee shop, which provided a much-needed distraction from my inner turmoil. The shop was a haven, a warm cocoon where I could momentarily escape the relentless torment of my thoughts. It was a safe space for me. I enjoyed crafting beautiful drinks; I loved their colors and flavors, and how they momentarily diverted me from my thoughts. Oddly, considering my dislike for coffee, I cherished that job. There, in the heart of that coffee-scented shop, people acknowledged my presence. Even if it was just to serve them their preferred brew, I felt genuinely appreciated.

My journey at that coffee shop had begun two years before, a mysterious pull drawing me into its radiant embrace. I had been hired online, never crossing paths with the elusive owner, yet a profound sense of belonging enveloped me within those walls. The shop—an intriguing blend of old-world charm and modernity—housed a treasure trove of aging books that adorned its shelves, although I seldom found the time to delve into them, despite my love for reading.

The coffee shop also included a fascinating assortment of relics from ages past, with ancient swords, weathered axes, and gleaming daggers that embellished rustic walls, each piece holding a story untold. Yet, it was the elaborately designed daggers that always captured my imagination. During those solitary moments late at night, as I prepared to close up shop, I found myself irresistibly drawn to them. My fingers would trace the finely detailed engravings on their handles, and in those moments, a sense of exhilaration would wash over me. In my solitude, I'd occasionally indulged in a whimsical notion, entertaining the idea that I possessed the power to move these ancient blades with nothing more than the sheer force of my mind.

The establishment offered impeccable Wi-Fi access, complemented by the exemplary customer service I took pride in providing as I managed the store. The owner had placed immense trust in me, granting the responsibility of running the shop five days a week and entrusting me with my own set of keys. That place felt more like a home than any other, and one evening, as I approached the end of my shift, I decided to challenge myself, timing how swiftly I could close up the shop.

Chapter 2: The Night, I Met Him

The night passed quickly. It was around 10:30–11 p.m., when I began my closing routine, that I heard a knock at the door, even though I'd had my headphones in, just loud enough to hear if someone approached. Setting the mop aside, I rushed to open the door. "We're closing in a few minutes. What can I get you?" I asked as the customer stepped inside, shedding his jacket.

He had dark eyes, a smooth face, and warm brown skin that seemed to please me. "Phew, I thought I'd missed you! I'll have a caramel coffee with whipped cream, please." He hung his coat on the rack and settled at the counter. I retreated behind the counter and started preparing his coffee in silence.

For a moment, the room was still. Then, he cleared his throat and said, "Why do they have you working so late? No one should be working alone at this hour."

I placed his coffee cup on the counter. I'm old enough to handle it, and nothing's ever happened."

He raised an eyebrow at me. "Are you always this quiet?"

I began adding caramel to his coffee. "Only around strangers." He grinned and introduced himself as "T." I nodded, saying, "Noted," and finished his coffee with whipped cream and a drizzle of caramel. When I slid the cup to him, our hands briefly touched. His skin felt both warm and cold, an intriguing contrast.

"Even when you're annoyed, your drinks turn out perfectly," he said.

I thanked him and resumed mopping the floor, and my curiosity about this "T" started growing. He also had me wondering how he knew I was annoyed. As I mopped, I thought to myself, *Who names their child just the letter "T?"* It was unusual, but I couldn't deny my interest.

When I finished my cleaning duties, he cleared his throat once more and said, "I'll wait for you outside while you finish locking up the store."

Well, that is shockingly amazing, I thought to myself. Afterward, I placed the mop back into the janitor's closet and washed out T's cup.

I checked the time; it was exactly 12:30 a.m. After securing the store, I placed the money in the safe assigned to my shift, turned off all the lights, and when I was finally locking the front door, I realized I'd lost my challenge to myself to lock up early because of the last customer. If only I could have mopped the floors and washed the dishes with my mind, it would have saved me time.

I honestly couldn't believe it! There he was again, waiting outside for me like he said he would. My curiosity deepened. What did this mysterious man want from me? Had he really stayed to ensure my safety?

"Can I at least know your name or what they call you?" he asked, taking my hand.

I sighed, saying, "My name is Venus."

"Like the planet. Noted." He grinned slightly to himself. I looked up and then our eyes met, like they'd finally arrived at their destination beneath the streetlight. Through his eyes, I could see his aura, shining like an angel. My heart raced, and I felt an inexplicable connection. After our name exchange, I got in my car and left, but I couldn't shake my thoughts of him as I drove home.

Surprisingly, my grandmother was awake when I arrived. For some reason, the last couple of days, my senses had been heightened, as if I knew sometimes how people felt or what they were going to say. So something in my mind kept saying *trip*. She informed me of her upcoming trip to Las Vegas with friends, and although I was happy for her, I couldn't muster much enthusiasm. My intuition seemed to be working overtime, telling me she had something important to share, but I kept my thoughts to myself.

"Hey, V," she said.

"Hey, Grandma."

She took a sip of her coffee and said, "I'm going on a girls' trip with a couple of my buddies. Do you remember Heather and Sharon?" she asked.

As I was taking off my work shoes, I said, "Yes, I do remember. Exactly where do you think you're going?"

She laughed out loud and said, "Oh honey, we're going to Vegas."

I picked up my shoes and said, "Have fun. I'll be here whenever you get back. Goodnight, Grandma." Las Vegas wasn't my ideal destination, so it didn't interest me. I had always dreamed of places like Washington, the Northern Lights, or Bora Bora; they piqued my interest and curiosity.

I walked inside my room, closed the door, and started to unwind. I took a deep breath, stretched my arms and cracked my fingers, undressed myself, tied my hair up, and walked into the bathroom. I grabbed my phone and started to play my favorite playlist, starting with the song, *Clouded*, by Brent Faiyaz. I turned the shower water on and got inside. As the water ran down my face, I started to think. I never thought about anyone, really; I was just in my own world. I never knew my parents, and since I felt no one never really acknowledge my presence, I didn't feel the presence of love. I never really thought about anyone else.

I mean, I feel they never cared for me or loved me, because they were never there. So was I wrong for feeling this way? *I am their child; I didn't ask to be here*, I said to myself. *Enough about them*, I thought as T rushed into mind.

I could sense his aura was different. Different from the auras I'd seen from other people. He couldn't be from here. *Who is he? Where is he from?* I pondered as I turned around and let the water hit my back. *What if I never see him again?*

My eyes flew open. "No way." I turned off the water, got out of the shower, and wrapped my towel around myself. *Did he put a spell on me?* I asked myself as I giggled. When he'd touched my hand, I'd felt electrified and had gotten chills at the same time.

"Pull yourself together, girl," I said while looking in the mirror at my brown skin, freckled face, and curly black hair. I turned to the side and walked back into my room. I got dressed and laid down. *He's not thinking about you, Venus*, were my last thoughts as I rolled over, smashing my face into my pillow, then falling to sleep.

Chapter 3: What a Day!

When I woke up the next morning, grandma was already gone. She had left a note on the counter top saying: *I left some food for you in the fridge. See you when I get back.* I crumbled up the piece of paper and threw it away. I opened the fridge and poured myself a cup of orange juice. "I guess I'll check the fair out today." I was off from work, but before going to the fair, I had to run a couple of errands.

I got dressed in a simple outfit and straightened my hair. I figured I should, since it was naturally curly and I wanted to look different today. Then I left the house. My first stop was going to the library to get a couple of books to read. Reading was one of my hobbies, as well as coloring-in books. Those activities were a safe space in my comfort zone and a way for me to connect with my inner child.

When I got to the library, Ms. Amber—the librarian—was there, waiting for me with a big smile on her face. By just looking at that sweet ol' lady and feeling her aura, I could tell she was someone's sweet, loving grandmother. "Hey, Venus. I haven't seen you here in a while. Come here and give me some love."

I gave Ms. Amber a big, warm hug and said, "I'm fine, Ms. Amber."

She lifted my head up and said, "Smile, Venus. I'm not going to make you tell me anything, but everything is going to be just fine."

I smiled and said, "Thanks Ms. Amber."

She rubbed her hands up against my shoulders and said, "I have some books I think you'll be interested in." She showed me the books and told me to bring them back whenever I was done with them. I gave Ms. Amber one last hug and left the library.

Ms. Amber was the type of woman I wish I'd had for a grandmother. Ms. Amber was always loving, and for that, she was one of the people most special to me.

After the library, I had to run to the store to buy a couple of snacks to eat while Grandma was gone, even though she'd left me food in the fridge I absolutely wasn't going to eat. I didn't plan on cooking anything while she was gone either. When I finally made it to the store, I grabbed a few things. Some Ritz crackers, pistachios, three bottles of Fiji water, and some Toms barbecue chips. When I made it to checkout, there was a long line ahead of me. Since I didn't have much patience, just standing there was starting to irritate me. Then, all of a sudden, I wasn't the last person in line anymore.

"Hello, Venus," I heard a deep voice say. I thought I recognized it, so I turned around and saw it was *him*.

I pulled my hair behind my ear and said, "Hello, T. It's a surprise to see you here." I noticed he wasn't wearing a coat that day. He was wearing a muscle T-shirt and some gray sweatpants. He didn't have much food in his shopping cart. It looked as if he was going to make ramen or some kind of Alfredo from what I could see.

He saw me looking at his grocery cart and said, "Would you like to join me?"

I looked at him, blushing, and said, "I'm going to the fair tonight. Would you like to join me?"

He placed his hand on his chin and looked me up and down like he'd done the first time he'd seen me. Then someone yelled, "Stop flirting and move up; the lines moving, kids!"

We laughed and then he said, "I'll take you to the fair tonight if you let me cook for you?"

"So, a date?" I said, calmly.

"I suppose so," he said excitedly.

After we were both checked out, he proceeded to help me with the things that were inside my cart, smiled, and said, "We have a date." T then walked me to my car. We were talking about all the rides he wanted to go on. When we made it to my car, we exchanged numbers. He opened the car door for me and said, "Drive safe, Venus. I'll be there to pick you up at around 7 tonight."

I smiled and said, "Goodbye, T."

I waited for him to walk a few cars down from mine, and when I saw him fading into the distance, I had a teenage girl moment full of excitement. My crush had just asked me out, helped with my groceries, and wanted to cook for me. I had all types of love butterflies flying in my stomach and around my head. But because I was the type of girl who stayed to herself and was always in her own mind, I also felt kind of weird. *Why me?*

I left the store and drove back home. I packed my snacks away and walked into my room. I paced back and forth because I didn't know what was going to happen tonight; I was always thinking. It was 5 p.m., so I decided to take a shower, do my hair, and settle on what kind of lip-liner I was going to wear that night. I didn't wear makeup because makeup, to me, just covered the bad parts of your face, and if people were going to like me, then they needed to see my real face.

After that, I got dressed and texted T. *Are we're still on for our date?* Not even one minute later—maybe even 30 seconds,—he texted back.

Of course we are. I'm getting ready now. Then I started to wonder, *Where is he coming from? Will he get here on time, or will he be late for our first date?* Then, he texted me again. *Send me your address.* I took a deep breath and gathered myself because I was nervous about sharing my location with him. He was still kind of a stranger. I thought to myself, *Is he really different from other guys or am I just yearning for someone to actually love me?* I placed my phone down and grabbed a pair of socks from the closet, a nice pair of sneakers, my purse, and a pack of Ritz crackers. Finally, I grabbed my lip-gloss to make my lip-liner pop, and my favorite perfume that made me smell like fresh flowers.

Then, my text message notification rang. *I'm outside.* Wow, he had come a few minutes earlier and was on time. It was 6:45 p.m., so I grabbed my keys, shut my room door, and left the house.

Chapter 4:
The Fair

When I got outside, I walked to the car and got in. I noticed that the car was all black on the outside, but the interior was all red. Black was my favorite color. He looked at me with his dark eyes, grinned, and said, "You look nice tonight, Venus."

I smiled and said, "Thank you." I would've told him he looked nice, but I'd be lying. He actually looked beautiful. He had on a black fitted T-shirt and some black sweatpants with a nice pair of sneakers as well. I was a sneaker-head, so I always notice someone's shoes. He had on a pair of earrings I thought were cute and some cologne that made him smell like a fresh hot spring.

He turned the air down and started to play a song. Luckily for me, I knew the song he was playing—*Chanel* by Frank Ocean. He turned the music up and then backed out of the driveway. We were on our way to the fair, and riding with him felt so peaceful. I felt really comfortable. While looking at him, I saw that he was even more angelic from the side. He had a buzz cut fade with a sharp tape up, a defined nose, and smooth skin. I wanted to touch him, but everyone had their own personal bubble, so I dared not to disturb.

Finally, we arrived. I started to open the door, but before I could fully open it, he placed his elbow on the console of his car and said, "Don't open that door, Venus." He clenched his jaw together.

"Okay, Mr. Gentleman," I said to him while blushing. He turned off the car and opened his door to let himself out. Then, he came to my side and opened my door. While getting out of the car, I looked up at him and noticed our height difference. He was tall—really tall. Though, that was probably an exaggeration because of how short I actually was.

I grabbed my purse, then he closed the door. We walked into the fair, and while we were in line to pay for our tickets, he turned to me and said, "Since this is our first date, can you to tell me more about yourself?"

I turned toward him and asked, "Well, what would you like to know?" Then it was silent.

It was our turn to pay for our tickets. "Two, please," he said with a grin on his face. When we walked into the fair, he stopped in the middle and said, "I want to know everything." He was standing there with a serious look. His hands were in his pockets and his head tilted, but holding it up so highly. Then, he grabbed my hand and said, "Let's start with the Ferris wheel." He grabbed my hand so smoothly. When he grabbed it, I felt electricity. My body heated up. I wondered if he could feel it too or could he feel how fast my body had turned warm.

I looked up at him as he looked straight ahead. *Is this really real or am I in a dream?* I thought. We approached the Ferris wheel ride, and the line wasn't that long, so we didn't have much time to wait. We got onto the ride, then he leaned his body over toward me and said, "I'm listening."

I smiled and said, "Well, my favorite color is black. I like to read and, of course, you already know that I work at the coffee shop." For some reason, I started to get nervous, so I began to rub my hands together. "I also like to watch movies every once in a while."

He raised his eyebrows. "What kind of movies?"

I cleared my throat and said, "I like to watch children's movies and horror movies, television series, and anime."

He grinned and said, "Continue." We were at the top of the sky at that point on the Ferris wheel. As he grabbed my hand again, I saw the glimmer in his eyes. *Wow*, I said to myself as he memorized me, not even focusing on the ride. He said, "You're very interesting. I know there's a lot more to you and I want to take the time to get to know you."

He then told me his favorite color was green. He liked to do pottery and drawings, which told me he was very creative. He also added he liked to watch movies as well, such as Marvel movies, anime, and children's movies. I guessed that was his way of interacting with his inner child.

We got off the ride and then walked around some more. My intuition was telling me there was a ride T would be scared on, but I paid it no mind, for I was living in the moment.

While walking, I saw a teddy bear I wanted. He looked down at me and said, "I'll win it for you." Then he winked at me.

The man who was hosting the game started to talk trash into his microphone. "He thinks he's going to win a present for his lovely girlfriend here tonight, folks."

I laughed and then shoved T. He looked at me and I smiled and said, "Win it for me." Then winked back at him. The man laughed and started to talk some more, but before he did, T threw the ball into the hole for the teddy bear I wanted. I smiled and said, "Thank you."

Then, we got on another ride—The Devil Below. This was the ride that scared T. I laughed because he was screaming a little bit too loudly, and that deep voice had gotten pretty low. When the ride was over with, he looked at me with a sad face and said, "We're never getting on that again." We both began to laugh. I thought to myself, *Wow, my intuition was right*. Then, I was the one who grabbed his hand. He clenched his jaw and interlocked his fingers with mine. He cleared his throat and asked me if I was I ready to eat.

I told him I was, but before we left, I bought a funnel cake. They were so good and I just had to have one. We walked out of the fair and walked to the car. He laughed and said, "You're so tiny."

I made an angry face and said, "Don't talk about my height."

He grabbed his chin and asked, "Insecurity?"

I pulled my hair back. "No." I was lying. I didn't like when anybody brought up my height or my weight. It was just something I never wanted to talk about.

Finally, we approached his car, and he opened the door for me as I got in. Upon arriving at the fair, T had insisted on being the perfect gentleman. He'd opened doors, made me laugh, and had won me a teddy bear at a game stall. Our connection grew stronger with every moment, and I felt a warmth I hadn't experienced before. My senses seemed to be hypersensitive whenever I was around him.

His house wasn't that far away from the fair. We pulled into his driveway, and before we got out of the car, he asked me, "Are you afraid of dogs?" I shook my head. I loved dogs, but I didn't have one. He exhaled a deep breath and said, "Whew, I thought you would be." I rolled my eyes and started to open my own door, but before I could, he quickly pulled me away from the door and said, "I will open the door for you; get that in your head." Then he pushed me, making me sit all the way back. He got out of the car and pointed at me while walking toward my side. "There you go, ma'am," he said.

I sucked my teeth. "Come on and show me around, Mr. Gentleman!"

Chapter 5: T's Home

As we approached his doorstep, the distant sound of his barking dog filled the air. "It's me, Ash," he said, reassuring his canine companion, opening the door and casting light into the spacious yet inviting interior. Gray walls, lush plants, and comfortable chairs greeted us. He guided me into the kitchen before disappearing briefly. When he returned, a blue-nosed pit bull named Ash accompanied him. He beamed at me, saying, "Ash, meet Venus. Venus, meet Ash." I kneeled down and rubbed Ash all over while T washed his hands, promising to show me his room after cooking.

I nodded, while still playing with Ash. T handed me the remote, saying, "YouTube or Netflix? Your choice."

I smiled and said, "Our music tastes align somewhat, but I'll let you be the judge of that."

He grinned and joked, "Please spare Ash and my eardrums from any harm." Laughter filled the room as I pulled up YouTube. As T was watching the boiling noodles, the song *One Night Only* by Sunder began to play, and he grooved to the rhythm. He started nodding his head and body to the beat.

I joined him in the kitchen. "I guess your eardrums appreciate it." He glanced at me with a hint of intrigue, then started to sing along. I rolled my eyes playfully. *No way! This guy knows every song.*

While the noodles simmered, T pulled me up onto the counter. "What's on your mind, Venus?"

I tilted my head, locking eyes with him, and replied calmly. "Nothing."

He sensed something amiss. "There must be something bothering you; you're in a stranger's house."

I rolled my eyes and crossed my legs. "Well, you did ask a stranger out on a date." His crooked smile captivated me; it seemed to hold some deeper meaning, much like my own smile, concealing past experiences.

Returning his attention to the cooking, T said, "It'll be ready in a few minutes." I hopped down from the counter, asking about the bathroom's location. He directed me down the hallway, and I smiled in thanks before proceeding. As I walked down the hallway, an odd sensation—a hyper sense, or some sort of psychic sensation—enveloped me as I approached the restroom's doorway. Taking a deep breath, I entered, but heard unsettling voices, whispering thoughts into my mind.

He's not who you think he is.

Do you know who you truly are?

It's almost time!

What the hell was that supposed to mean? I mean, why was I hearing these things? I splashed water on my face, closed my eyes, and drew another deep breath. It felt like my lungs were struggling under the weight of those voices.

I hurriedly opened the door, and in the hallway, I found T placing our food on plates. He noticed my watchful gaze and offered a friendly grin. I smiled oddly and approached him, intrigued but cautious. "You look as if you just heard a ghost or something."

I laughed softly and said, "Not a ghost, but I did hear some voices."

He looked confused, but started laughing because he thought I was joking. T grabbed two forks and the remote. "Care to join me?" I returned the smile, sliding my hands behind my back, and followed him into the living room. He peered at me somewhat nervously, as if sensing my unease.

I cleared my throat. "I enjoy a bit of everything—anime, horror, action, dramas, and, of course, romance." His gaze delved deeper into my eyes as I spoke.

He handed me my plate, nodding appreciatively. T selected the movie *Warm Bodies*, a story about a world divided between humans and zombies, with a zombie named R and a human girl named Julie. The movie was engrossing, and made you think, "What if zombies were real?" T's cooking proved equally delightful. We finished our meals quickly while engaging in the movie. Talking during a good movie really irked me, and it seemed T shared this sentiment. We lounged on the sofa, enjoying the remainder of the movie. This caused me to almost forget about the bathroom incident. He glanced at me several times, but we spoke little, which suited me perfectly. The tension in the air was even more noticeable, enhanced by the cinematic experience.

As the movie neared its conclusion, I felt a bit of sadness, though the satisfying ending offered some solace. I wondered if they'd ever make a sequel. Once the credits rolled, T gently moved my legs aside and collected our plates. "Did you enjoy it?" he asked. I sat up, realizing it was getting late, but I was having a good time, despite my lingering suspicions about this unfamiliar place, the voices I'd heard, and the fact he'd never showed me his room.

"It was delicious." I checked my phone. Time had flown by, but being here felt right, even though I was aware of the underlying mystery.

T placed the dishes in the sink and rejoined me. Standing before me, he parted my legs and inched closer. "Don't you think it's getting late?" he asked, his touch sending warmth through my body. I scooted back in the chair, revealing that my grandmother was out of town. His hands rested on my thighs, and a peculiar sensation washed over me. I sensed he felt the heat radiating from my body. His gaze locked onto mine as he murmured, "I enjoyed your company. Maybe you could come back?" My heart raced, and I contemplated a kiss, but it was our first night together, and he remained a stranger. He gently grasped my chin. "I really enjoyed your company tonight."

I responded with a smile, blinking a few times before replying. "I enjoyed you too, and your house is lovely." Inwardly, I questioned my choice of words, but his crooked smile hinted at a deeper connection.

We walked to the car together, then he opened the passenger door for me. Once we were situated in the car, he started to play the song *Care* by Sunder. He placed his hand on my thigh again. He kept it there the whole way to my grandmother's house. When we pulled into the driveway, he looked at me with his dark, glistening eyes. His lips seemed to be calling out to mine. T tucked a strand of hair behind my ear. "Could I see you tomorrow?"

I met his gaze and said, "Sure." Although an urge to kiss him surged within me, I resisted, not wanting to complicate our budding connection. I opened the door and let myself out.

T waited until I'd safely entered my grandmother's house before leaving. I locked the door and texted him, *Be safe*. It seemed like the considerate thing to do after he'd waited for me to enter. Inside my room, I took a deep breath, grappling with unfamiliar emotions and the enigmatic bathroom incident. I undressed and prepared for a bath, needing to reflect on the surreal experiences of the evening. As the tub filled with water, I pondered the intrusive thoughts and voices I had heard. *Could they be his? Who were they? What were they trying to tell me?* I wondered. Questions swirled in my mind, but I couldn't bring myself to ask. Perhaps it was fear, or maybe I didn't want to burden him. The water offered a soothing escape as I splashed it on my face, vowing that the truth would reveal itself in due time.

I grabbed my towel and phone, discovering two messages from T. *You're on my mind heavily right now*, and *It's like your presence is still here*. I dropped my phone momentarily, staring at myself in the mirror, then picked it up and placed it on my dresser. A scream of frustration escaped my lips before I composed myself. He was a stranger; someone I'd known for only two days. I finally replied, *You get to see me tomorrow, but I shouldn't be on your mind right now*, I knew I had been thinking about him too, but admitting it felt like vulnerability I wasn't ready to show. As my racing heart began to calm, I turned over and drifted into sleep.

Chapter 6: Who Am I?

The next morning, T hadn't responded to my message. I began my day in my grandmother's kitchen, checking the available supplies. Fortunately, she had brought my favorite cereal and some frozen foods. After a quick cereal breakfast, I brushed my teeth, pondering what to do while waiting for T's reply. As I put on my pants, my phone chimed with a message from him. *Sorry about last night. I just couldn't help but tell you what was actually on my mind*, he wrote, sounding apologetic. A blush crept onto my cheeks as I read it. While I was cautious about relationships and love, I viewed our time together as a chance to enjoy the experience.

Without hesitation, I decided to call him. He answered with a raspy voice, likely still lying down. I quickly got to the point. "I'm heading to the library today. You can join me if you'd like." His raspy voice disappeared instantly as he cleared his throat and inquired about the time. I chuckled, replying, "Right now, T." I could sense his grin through the phone. He may have seemed mysterious, but it felt like he needed someone to bring out his inner child. Still, I couldn't prioritize his needs above my own; that was a line I wouldn't cross.

Before leaving my grandmother's house, I grabbed a bottle of water, two oatmeal pies—one for myself and one for T—and lastly, my car keys. *I hope he'll let me read to him at the library*, I thought to myself. On the way there, I played the song *Awkward* by SZA; its smooth melody was calming my thoughts. I pondered our connection. Was it fate? I didn't believe in love at first sight, but I recognized a certain chemistry between us. This feeling was weird and confusing. It was time to address it; I didn't want it to taint my view of him as a friend. After all, friends shared the truth with each other, right?

Upon arriving at the library, I found T waiting in his car. I parked and approached his driver's window, tapping on it. "Get out of the car now," I said playfully.

He nodded, saying, "Pushy much?" with a smirk on his face.

I grabbed his hand and earnestly said, "Come on," as we entered the library.

Inside, we encountered Ms. Amber, with her welcoming smile that always lit up the room. She asked with curiosity, "Hi Venus, who's the lucky guy?"

I introduced T, and then said, "T, this is Ms. Amber, the librarian." Then she humorously warned him to take care of me, threatening to smash him into little pieces with the library books if he didn't. Ms. Amber was my guardian angel and protector. We laughed, and I thanked her before leading T to my usual spot. His shocked expression, likely prompted by the old lady's humorous threat, didn't go unnoticed, and I laughed.

It was time to address the matter at hand. We sat down, and I handed him an oatmeal pie from my tote bag. "For me?" he asked.

I politely replied, "Of course." He placed it beside him, and I retrieved the book I wanted to read aloud: *One of Us Is Lying* by Karen M. McManus. It was a mystery about classmates suspected of their peer's death, each with hidden secrets. Before I began, I took a moment to look at T. I stared at him, examining his features, until he tilted his head, leaned into his beanbag chair, and locked eyes with mine.

"You're very beautiful," he said in his deep, raspy voice, his eyes transmitting an unspoken connection. I thanked him, but my questions couldn't wait any longer. I wanted to know more. Before I could say anything, he gently grabbed my face, pulling me closer until our lips were almost touching. I thought he was going to kiss me, but instead, he brushed his thumb over my chin and held my hand, asking me not to freak out. I promised I wouldn't, sealing it with a pinky promise. He smiled and straightened up, ready to share something important.

"Your parents aren't who you think they are, Venus," were the first words that came out of his mouth. I nodded, confused, wanting to laugh, but I allow him to continue. *How does he even know my parents?* "It may sound weird or funny, but it's the truth," he said with the oddest straightest face I ever seen. So I began to take him seriously as he continued talking.

"Mr. and Mrs. Stone were vampires. Your mother, once human, and I believe to be a psychic, was pregnant with you when I first met her. She was my nanny. She as very beautiful, caring, and nice. She told me many stories I thought at the time were just stories. Your dad, however, was what you called a Ripper—a warrior vampire who enjoys mutilating their victims and known for his brutality, but somehow controlled himself with your mother. I believe it was because of the qualities your mother possessed. The last time I saw your mother, she looked as if she was in a fight with another animal and had bite marks on her arm and legs. Your mother saw me and told me to pinky promise that I would watch over her daughter, Venus Stone, and treat her the way she treated me. Venus, do you hear voices or feel you have any psychic abilities? You are still half vampire and half human."

Wow. What? I was so confused. So, T had met both my parents. According to him, my mother had instructed him to find me and look after me when I grew up. T revealed he had known my parents even before my birth, painting a bizarre picture of them as vampires. *Wait, how old is T?* His words left me puzzled, and he dropped an even more shocking revelation: I could hear voices and have psychic abilities because I was "still" half vampire and half human. What did "still" mean? My mind raced with questions and uncertainty. I decided I needed to discuss this with my grandmother when she returned from her trip. Was this truth being hidden from me? Was T actually telling me the truth? Who were my parents, actually? Was this the reason I had heard those voices at his house, or the reason I had felt I could move those daggers at work with my mind? All sorts of questions kept flooding into my mind, and I needed some clarity.

CHAPTER 7:
A CHOICE TO EMBRACE

T continued to speak about the situation. "The only path to becoming a full vampire is by drinking blood, but it's your decision.

My eyes welled with tears, and I fought to prevent them from spilling. *I could become a vampire*, I thought. I rested in his lap as he continued, shedding light on drinking blood in order to awaken my vampire side.

"I'm sorry. I should have reached out to you sooner, interacted more," he said, causing my eyes to moisten.

In the library, I couldn't scream, show aggression, or let a single tear fall. He pulled me close, wiping away my tears before they had a chance to escape. His whispered apology touched my heart deeply as I rested my head on his chest. "So, what do you feed on?"

He took a deep breath and said, "Later," and wrapped me in his arms. *Is T some sort of vampire as well?*

I sniffled a few times and started to do what I had come there to do. I tried to continue to act normal even though T had just hit me with some confusing, unannounced, shocking to the core information. I started reading a chapter from the book I'd wanted to read T. While T was lying beside me, our breaths seem to synchronize, creating a strangely normal but comforting atmosphere. When I neared the end of the chapter, T tugged my hair behind my ear and said, "It's time to go home."

I glanced at him, curious, and asked, "Home?" He remained silent. As I reached the final page, I stood and said, "Let's go." I was uncertain about his sudden seriousness; he seemed like someone who could switch from lighthearted to intense in an instant. Before leaving the library, I bid farewell to Ms. Amber, and as I glanced back at T, I noticed her scrutinizing him, bringing some much-needed laughter to me as we left the library.

Outside, T said, "My car can stay here; I'll ride with you."

Of course, I thought, unlocking the car door and observing his demeanor as he got in. He was calm and didn't reveal any anger; it seemed like he had more important information to discuss. Inside the car, I played *Cameras* by Drake. T stared out the window with his seat reclined, bobbing his head and tapping his fingers to the rhythm. Then, he sighed and took a deep breath, different from before, as if he were struggling to breathe, breathing too rapidly. His hand rested firmly on my thigh with increasing force and aggression. I said nothing all the way home.

When we arrived home, he stepped out of the car while it was still in drive, waiting for me to come to a full stop before opening my door. I locked the car doors behind me, sensing his closeness. He locked the front door, and to break the tension, I offered him water. "Sure," he said with a cleared throat. I fetched two bottles and led the way to my room, since T had never shown me his room. As I opened the door, I peeked back to ensure he appreciated the unique ambiance of my room.

It was adorned with exit signs, paintings, a couch, a computer, and black walls. His grin upon entering made me smile. He pushed the door closed. "I've only had human food once before, and when you left from dinner the other night, I had a bad stomachache," he said, answering the question I'd asked at the library. Then, he revealed his true nature. "I live off human blood, Venus."

My heart raced, but strangely, fear wasn't the dominant emotion. I wanted to hug him, even after learning this. His fangs appeared, and his eyes turned a menacing gray, filled with sadness and aggression. He looked like he could snap your neck like a pencil, but at the same time, show signs of compassion. He stepped closer. "Would you still care to get to know me even when I look like this?"

I gently rubbed his face and assured him, "Of course, T." Shockingly, I wasn't scared of him at all. He returned to his normal appearance, and I took a deep breath, sitting on my bed.

T lowered his head, waiting for me to speak. I inched closer, playfully tapping the back of his head before embracing him. "I just wish you had told me a little bit earlier, you know?" I said. He hugged me tighter and apologized. He pulled away and tucked a strand of hair behind my ear.

"Can I stay with you?" he asked, and I agreed, even though I wasn't sure if it was a good idea. I needed him here; discovering the truth about myself had been painful. He cleared his throat and hugged me again. "It's only us, Venus." I hugged him tighter, resting my head on his chest.

I gazed up and asked, "What would happen if I were to become a full vampire?"

He took my chin gently. "We'll leave." A soft smile spread across my face, and we both knew this was the beginning of a new chapter in our lives.

Chapter 8:
More of the Unknown

T settled onto the bed. "I need to grab some fresh clothes from my place."

I nodded. "I understand." I tossed him my car keys. "You're driving." After securing my house, we embarked on the journey to his.

As we drove, my eyes welled with tears, overwhelmed by the gravity of the situation. This was a journey I wasn't sure I could navigate alone; at this point, I needed him, even though I didn't know his real name or birthday—or many other things, for that matter. My head began to throb. He reached out, gently pulling my arm and lifting my spirits. "We're almost there, Venus. You can relax when we get back to your place." A sly grin formed on his face. My mind raced with questions. What was he planning?

I couldn't help but ponder how tonight would unfold. He was staying with me, and he'd be there when I'd woken up. It all felt incredibly rushed. Glancing toward the front door of his home, I saw him standing there. After locking the door, he returned to the car. "Missed me?" he asked.

I grinned. "Come on, it's getting late."

Upon our return, I noticed a black Honda parked in the driveway, and dread washed over me. My grandmother. T turned off the car and asked, "Weren't expecting any guests?" I sighed and opened the passenger's door. Turning to him, I extended my hand, and he walked toward me, clasping it. Together, we headed for the front door.

Inside, we found my grandmother and her friends in the kitchen. I moved toward my grandmother, attempting to introduce her to T, but she forcefully pushed me aside and interrogated T. "Why show up now?"

T cleared his throat. "We can discuss this after your company leaves." My grandmother's ears reddened, torn between anger and politeness. She took a deep breath and apologized to me, then redirected her attention to her friends, talking about their trip. *Does T know my grandmother? What is going on?*

"How was the trip?" I asked.

Tammy and Paula smiled and said, "Oh, it was wonderful, Venus. Maybe you should come next time."

I gave them a half smile and awkwardly said, "Of course." I finished the introductions, pulling T toward me and saying, "T, meet Tammy and Paula; Tammy and Paula, meet T."

Teasingly, Tammy said, "You're a fine young man."

"You don't know when to stop, Tammy. He's clearly too young for you," Paula said. They playfully assessed T and me.

Then, I led T to my room while my grandmother and her friends exchanged hushed comments. "Well, at least she's seeing someone, Clair," Tammy said.

"I don't know if he's the best for her," my grandmother said.

I shut my room door and sighed. "My grandma must hate you."

T leaned against the wall. "It seems there's some animosity."

We gazed at each other until we heard the front door shut, signifying the departure of my grandmother's friends. A minute later, she knocked on my door, and T answered. My grandmother entered, standing in the middle of the room. "Now, answer my question: why now?" she asked.

T stood upright. "She's older now."

My grandmother turned to me. "Do you want to become a vampire?"

My surprise was evident as I stammered, "You knew and didn't tell—"

"It's not about not telling you. I did what I believed was best for you, Venus. Be grateful."

I stood up. "Well, I need time to think." Frustration mounted, causing my grandmother's ears to redden once more.

T stepped back. "I should've been here for Venus earlier."

My grandmother began to cry, her emotions raw. "It's not about being here early; it's about the demon you'll awaken if she agrees."

Outraged, I confronted my grandmother. "A demon? You think I'll become a demon!" Our relationship had been distant, but that day, with T staying over, tensions flared. I composed myself, apologized, then gathered my belongings and retreated to the bathroom. Sitting with my head between my legs, I stared at the bamboo floor, tears streaming down my face. Numbness had overtaken me, leaving me questioning why this was happening to me. *Why are there so many things I do not know about myself or my life? How the hell does T know my grandmother?*

I stood up, wiped my eyes, and studied my reflection in the mirror, my eyes tired and hair disheveled. A knock at the door interrupted my thoughts. "Open up for me, Venus," T said. Sniffling, I unlocked the door, and he swept me toward the bathroom counter with surprising speed. My legs wrapped around him, our eyes locking intensely. "We don't have to stay here if you're upset or uncomfortable."

I was speechless, grappling with the revelation of him being a vampire. He gently lifted my chin and caressed my thighs. Without thinking, I pulled him close, and we kissed. *Wow.* It was my first kiss, under all this stress, but it wonderfully wowed me. He pulled away but, compelled by desire, I tugged him back, insisting he stay with me. Hopping down from the counter, I undressed, remarkably comfortable with him despite the surreal circumstances. "Is this weird?" I wondered and accidentally said out loud.

"It's not weird."

I turned on the shower, letting the water flow while contemplating his reaction when I stepped out. After turning off the water, I grabbed a towel, pulled back the shower curtain, and saw T leaning against the bathroom counter, his face turned away. I chuckled and teasingly said, "Respect points."

He laughed. "Hurry up. I'm tired of not being able to look at you." I dried off and changed into my nightgown, releasing my hair.

"You can look at me now," I said. When he gazed at me, his ears perked up, and his fangs emerged.

"You're very beautiful, Venus," he murmured, moving closer, his hands on my waist. "Do you want to stay or leave?"

As we stood there, the mutual feelings between us were tangible. I hesitated before speaking again. "I need a minute to talk with my grandmother first, T." He took hold of my shoulders, stepped aside, and opened the door.

He retreated to my bedroom, and I knew I had to have a conversation with my grandmother. I shouldn't have raised my voice earlier. I walked into her room and asked if we could talk. She sighed and sat up in bed, forgiving me and emphasizing her concern for my safety. I placed my hands on hers, telling her I loved her, and that wouldn't change even if I became a vampire. We hugged, and she asked if T was my boyfriend.

I laughed. "We're just friends."

My grandmother, ever perceptive, side-eyed me. "I was born at night, but not last night, Venus." I grinned and rolled my eyes before returning to my room.

I pressed my body against T, who rubbed my shoulders. "Let's stay here tonight," he said, wrapping me in his embrace.

Chapter 9: Grandma Unveils the Truth

That morning, I awoke to find T absent from my room. Sliding the covers aside, I ventured down the hallway toward my grandmother's room, where she still lay in slumber. My path then led me to the bathroom; its door was closed. Though I always knocked before entering, as my hand approached the door, it unexpectedly swung open. "Finally, you're awake," he said.

I smiled in response. "I woke up and didn't see you." He gently pushed me against the wall, planting a kiss on my neck before inquiring about my return to work. I sighed. "Tomorrow."

With that, he scooped me up and said, "Well, let's go for a ride then."

A grin crossed my face, and I agreed. "Okay."

Upon opening the bathroom door, we were met with an unexpected sight. My grandmother stood in the middle of the hallway, her arms folded, and her foot tapping impatiently. I eyed her up and down and allowed my arms to fall limply to my sides. "What's the matter now, Grandma?" I asked.

She rolled her eyes. "Hurry up and get him out of my house."

T stepped forward and cleared his throat. "What do I have to do to make you like me?"

Words I had never heard my grandmother utter before spilled from her lips in that very moment. "Die. Burn in hell like my daughter and her selfish husband did!" she yelled. "You think just because Venus is doing fine now that she's older, you can come in and sweep her off her feet?" She drew me closer. "I raised her as a human because I don't know what kind of life she'd be stepping into. There's so much she doesn't know and so many things I need to tell her. She needs to know everything before making her own decision." My grandmother locked her teary brown eyes onto mine. "Venus, promise me something." I glanced at her, nodding my head slightly in response. Before she could articulate her request, a car pulled into the driveway. My grandmother cleared her throat. "I wonder who that could be?"

I shrugged my shoulders and peered out the nearest window through the curtains. "There's no one there." The vehicle remained, but its driver was conspicuously absent. T swiftly circled the entire house, trying to verify that everything was secure and locked.

Meanwhile, my grandmother paced anxiously. "I knew he was up to no good; you two can't be together!" she shouted.

T raised his voice in response. "Shh! Someone is out there, and I can't sense them, so they must be a vampire."

What if someone is after me? I thought to myself. T then gazed at me, his concern mirroring my own thoughts.

I moved closer to my grandmother, intending to express my understanding of her worries and frustration. To tell her I need answers because I was lost and for her to tell me what was going on. However, before I could utter a word, a gunshot rang out, but I could see it, as if it were moving in slow motion. It shattered through the glass, then rapidly through our old bookshelf by the window, then I saw it enter the room where we were standing. *I can dodge it, but if I move, it will hit my grandmother.* So I stayed in front of my grandmother and the bullet pierced my ribcage.

CHAPTER 10: T'S MIND BEGAN TO RACE

"Venus, my love." My heart raced as I gently laid her down, then I darted through the entire house. Questions raced through my mind. Who were they? Why had they done this? Fury, death, and anger were coursing through my veins. Whoever was responsible for this would pay, no matter the cost.

Meanwhile, Venus's grandmother scooped her up, rushing to take her to the hospital. As I reached the outside, I found him—the person behind this attack. "Lucky."

When our eyes met, he grinned. "Missed me?" Lucky, a vicious vampire, had vanished from my life when we were children. I couldn't help but wonder what had brought him back.

My fangs extended as I approached him, trying to determine his intentions. "What brings you here?" I asked.

"Taki, you're falling for the wrong girl. Everyone is looking for her, and you know it," Lucky said. "I have to do what must be done and bring her in."

As I pondered how to kill him and who had sent him, I suddenly heard the sound of Venus and her grandmother pulling out of the driveway. But Lucky remained too preoccupied with me to notice their departure. "I need to be with her," I said.

Lucky laughed. "She's not going to make it. I'm going to capture her, and killing you, Taki, would just be an added bonus…"

I stared into his eyes and smiled. A surge of newfound power washed over me, unlike anything I'd ever felt. As I moved closer to him, two shots sprung out, but he missed, and my hands penetrated his body as I gripped his still-beating heart. "Lucky, who sent you here? Why did you shoot her? What is your plan?" I asked him angrily.

His body trembled, and on the brink of death, he muttered something. "If you don't hide her now, they'll come for you, her, and her grandmother." I tightened my grip, causing him to cough up blood. Then, he was gone. I severed his head from his body and set it ablaze. I had to set out to find where Venus's grandmother had taken her.

Once I reached the hospital where Venus was being treated, I rushed in to find her grandmother in the waiting room, tears streaming down her face. I approached her hastily. "Is she dead?" I asked, gripping my chest in anguish.

She gave me a stern look before responding. "They haven't said anything yet." I took a deep breath to regain control of my emotions. Closing my eyes, I focused on Venus's heartbeat, trying to hear it amidst the jarring of others in the hospital. Finally, I heard it— faint, but there. Her heart was barely beating. Deep down, I knew I could save her if she would choose to become a vampire, but that wasn't my true desire for Venus. I didn't mind if she chose to remain human, growing old alongside my children someday. It was up to Venus. She was unique, and although her grandmother feared she'd become a demon, I knew I could keep her sane.

A few moments later, the nurse emerged and called for Venus's grandmother. She stood up and approached the nurse. "Is she alive?" she asked, her voice trembling.

The nurse smiled. "Yes, ma'am. You can go see her now." Her grandmother turned and glanced at me, gesturing for me to accompany them. I wanted to smile broadly, but I refrained and followed the two of them. We reached Venus's room, and her grandmother entered alone. I waited outside, keeping a lookout, while observing Venus and her grandmother's interaction, remembering what Lucky had said about people trying to capture her. *I needed answers.*

"Is he here?" Venus asked her grandmother. Her heart skipped a beat when she saw me. She repositioned herself to sit up and extended her hands.

I leaned in for a warm hug, sensing her pain. I could hear the stifled sobs she held back. As I embraced her, I whispered in her ear, "I'm glad you're okay."

She smiled at me, then turned to her grandmother. "Don't be mad at him. It's not his fault."

Her grandmother's tears flowed freely as she looked at both of us. "I'm not mad at T," she said. "I'm mad at the consequences behind it. I'm mad because you are innocent and now you bear the sins of your parents. I'm mad because I wasn't able to keep you from knowing this life." I hung my head for a moment before interlocking my fingers with Venus's. She extended her other hand to her grandmother, who hesitated before finally taking a deep breath. "If you're willing to risk your life for someone who couldn't even tell you their real name, then do it. If you want to risk your life knowing nothing of your past, your parents, and now being shot at or hunted down, it's your choice! But I want no part of that type of life for you. I will always love you and be here for you. I'm just happy you are okay now. You're older now, so whatever happens from this day forward is your choice, your responsibility, and the consequences you will have to face on this journey with him."

Her grandmother offered Venus a final hug before leaving the hospital. She then turned to me and said, "I ask that you promise to at least keep her safe and at peace."

I nodded. "I will always love and protect Venus with my life." With those words, she departed.

Once her grandmother had left, Venus gazed at me, her eyes filled with determination and anger. "Are people after me? Is someone trying to kill me? What is your real name?" she asked. I held onto her fingers more firmly, confirming her suspicions. She pulled my face down to hers, clutching my cheeks with her hands. Her voice trembled, reminiscent of a child facing a daunting situation. I brushed her hair behind her ear and revealed my real name, Taki do Malone. She smiled. "Why didn't you tell me before?" I changed the subject, not wanting her to feel the urgency of the situation.

I looked into her eyes. "My name may be strange and somewhat amusing, but it was time for me to tell you." Inside, I feared losing Venus.

She traced her fingers down my back, then kissed me. "You won't let anything happen to me, right?" she asked.

I kissed her passionately. "I'll always be there for you. I'm never leaving your side."

A knock at the door interrupted our moment, and the doctor entered. "You must be her boyfriend," he said, glancing at Venus and me. Venus looked at me, arching an eyebrow as if to seek my reaction. The doctor cleared his throat, his gaze now serious. "Venus will be able to go home tomorrow morning." His words held an unusual tension and his eyes seemed compassionate with concern, with flashes of fire. It didn't take such a grave demeanor to convey such a simple message, but I understood his caution. After he left, Venus tapped my shoulder, questioning my thoughts.

"Do you think that was suspicious?" she asked.

I smiled. "It was. A serious gesture and a lot of tension for just a few words."

We exchanged knowing glances. "He's up to something," we said in unison.

I needed to get Venus out of here. *Maybe the doctor knows Lucky*, I thought to myself. I cupped the back of Venus's neck and drew her closer. "Let's disappear."

Her eyes widened, and she asked, "Are you serious?"

I grinned. "Just for a few days." I needed to get her to a safe place until I could find out what was going on and who'd sent Lucky after us.

Venus looked concerned and brought up her job at the coffee shop.

"What's wrong?" I sighed.

"I really liked working there; it was the only place that made me feel normal, that made me feel happy, and where my presence was felt." I kissed her forehead and assured her I would build her a coffee shop of her own one day. A radiant smile spread across Venus's face, causing a twinge of pain from her bruise.

She picked up the phone and began dialing her grandmother's number. "I just need to check on her," she said. I watched her, understanding her concern. Her grandmother answered, and Venus inquired about her condition. "I can see the doctor standing there; he's up to something," Venus said.

I hugged her. "I'll do anything to keep you safe." She laid back down, expressing her readiness to leave the hospital, and I tucked her hair behind her ear, reassuring her that she would be home tomorrow. "Get some rest, Venus. Don't worry." As Venus rested, I decided to venture out into the hallway to make sure she was secure.

CHAPTER 11: VENUS WAKE UP

My brush with death weighed heavily on my mind that morning as a laid in bed. *I could've died yesterday. What is going on? I need answers from everyone.* Those were among the few thoughts that were racing through my head. Everything was so frustrating. Taki do Malone's suggestion to disappear for a few days was a great one, and with all of this going on, my only excuse was the coffee shop. I mean, I loved working at the coffee shop, and even though my grandmother had raised me, the coffee shop had always felt like my home. Why did the coffee shop even matter? Now that I was half vampire, was in love with a vampire, my life had taken a decidedly supernatural turn. It was all so overwhelming.

Taki do Malone. His name was unique, but it had become special to me, just like he had. I knew other vampires and people would come for me, and the day would arrive when I had to make the most significant decision of my life. I felt a strange excitement about it all. After all, you only lived once in this vast universe. However, something still felt amiss, particularly regarding that suspicious doctor.

I gingerly placed my hand on my wounded rib, wincing slightly before carefully sliding out of the hospital bed and onto the floor. As I stood upright, T walked in through the door quickly, his eyes filled with excitement. "You're standing!" he exclaimed. "Let's go."

I smiled. "Sweep me away, my hero." He scooped me up and planted a kiss on my lips before we faded away. For an ordinary human, leaving the hospital in such a condition would be unthinkable, but since I was half vampire, I was willing to defy the odds.

Once we reached the car, the suspicious doctor was waiting for us. "I'm glad you stayed with her and took her out of the hospital, even though I know you sensed it to be a bit early for a patient in her condition," he said to Taki.

I pushed my hair behind my ear and exchanged a glance with T. He opened the passenger door to put me in while asking the doctor, "What do you want?" I could feel T getting ready to go on the offensive, trying to protect me. The man clenched his jaw before inquiring, "What do you want with this patient?" T scrutinized the man, then looked back at me and gave me a look that told me to get ready for what was about to happen next.

The man smiled and said, "Well, Taki, don't act like you don't remember me."

I held onto T's hand and whispered, "Stay by my side."

He turned toward me, his gaze filled with devotion. "I'm never leaving you."

The man approached the car and, as he drew nearer, cracked his neck from side to side. He then grinned and said, "I know it's been a long time, Venus, but I'm your father."

I cleared my throat and stood up, my blood bubbling. "What? Why come now? Where have you been? What happen to my mother?"

My father stared into my eyes. "Well, you certainly have my temper, but, darling, this is a serious matter." He leaned in closer. "You're in a lot of trouble, especially once the other vampires find out your name is Venus Stone. Take her out of the country for a few days," he said, his voice sharper and deeper.

T looked at me, pulling me closer to him. "I'm waiting for her to decide if she wants to go, Mr. Stone."

My father grinned. "You've grown to be a gentleman, I see, but you're still different, Taki." He leaned in, his tone darkening. "You're a vampire who is learning how much stronger you can be the deeper your love for someone is." T lowered his head, offering a fake ashamed smile. It was clear he didn't want me to know everything just yet. My father approached me, pulling my hair back gently. "Kiss your grandmother for me. It's time we all have a sit down to tell you everything that is going on. And she will come around. She knows how to kill vampires as well. I'm sorry for not coming to you sooner, my daughter." He then switched to a more unsettling tone. "Go get your grandmother, get out of town for a couple of days, and I will meet y'all there! I know how to find you! Take care of them, Taki!" Then, he vanished into thin air. It was astonishing how quickly he could move being a vampire.

Finally, finally, I can get the answers I'm looking for, so I can rid myself of all this confusion, anxiety, and mystery about myself, my past, and my parents! Then a loud noise started ranging in my head and I woke up! It was my alarm clock going off at 6:36 a.m. at the coffee shop! *What?! I'm still here? Did I fall asleep here last night? Was this all a dream, but it felt so real! I must have. Wow. Really, none of it was real. Why does it feel like that? Why do I remember every detail so vividly?* From my grandmother, to Taki, to even seeing my father. Even the gun-shot wound had felt real. Taki's love for me was strong because I could still feel his presence in my heart. *What is happening to me? Am I half vampire? Do I have psychic abilities? Are my parents alive?* It was time to talk to my grandmother. It was time to get answers about my past!

Printed in the USA
CPSIA information can be obtained
at www.ICGtesting.com
LVHW061122200224
772325LV00003B/54

9 798989 172351